A1
Scratch Your Brain

Clever Math Ticklers

SERIES TITLES:

SCRATCH YOUR BRAIN A1

SCRATCH YOUR BRAIN B1

SCRATCH YOUR BRAIN C1

SCRATCH YOUR BRAIN GEOMETRY

DOUG BRUMBAUGH

LINDA BRUMBAUGH

DAVID ROCK

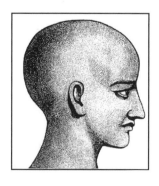

© 2001
THE CRITICAL THINKING CO.
(BRIGHT MINDS™)
www.CriticalThinking.com
P.O. Box 1610 • Seaside • CA 93955-1610
Phone 800-458-4849 • FAX 831-393-3277
ISBN 0-89455-788-2

This book contains 126 problems, all of which meet at least one of the standards set forth by the National Council of Teachers of Mathematics. Pages iv and v contain matrices that link each problem to its relevant standards. The problems are sequenced by difficulty throughout the book and each chapter. Chapter titles correspond to common textbook topics.

Many of the problems in this book also ask students to write explanations of how they got their answers. Scoring rubrics are included for each of these problems. Keep in mind that students will often come up with an answer that is not totally correct but still shows the thinking necessary to obtain the correct answer. Thus, a student could get "partial credit" even though the answer is not correct. This partial credit would be the recognition that the student was able to articulate through words and sentences the mathematical processes one would use to arrive at the correct answer.

For example, problem 34 on page 27 says this:

34. What number will come next?

2,   4,   6,   ____

Explain how you got your answer.

Here is a sample student answer:

"Each number gets bigger by two. Four is 2 + 2. Six is 4 + 2. So I added 2 to 6 and got 8."

Here is the rubric for this problem (page 84):
Rubric: 2 possible points
1 point (content): recognize pattern
1 point (clarity): explanation clearly written

The sample student answer recognizes the pattern and is also a clearly written explanation of how the student solved the problem. Thus, this answer would get the student the full 2 points. A student who recognized the pattern but did not clearly articulate his or her steps to solving the problem would be awarded 1 point. (At the teacher's discretion, 1 point *could* be awarded to a student who wrote a clear explanation of how he or she came up with an answer that was incorrect. This might not seem plausible on an easier problem such as this, but more difficult problems would easily lend themselves to this possibility.)

Note: There may occasionally be multiple solutions to a problem. If a student comes up with a solution that works, give credit even though that answer may not be listed.

CONTENTS

A1 MATHEMATICS

ACTIVITIES ACCORDING TO
NATIONAL MATHEMATICS STANDARDS

NCTM Standard	1	2	3	4	5	6	7	8	9	10	11	12	13	14	15	16	17	18	19	20	21	22	23	24	25
Number, Operation	■	■	■	■		■	■	■	■	■	■		■	■	■	■	■	■		■	■	■	■	■	■
Algebra				■									■					■				■			
Geometry														■											
Measurement							■	■			■	■							■		■		■		
Data Analysis, Probability																									
Problem Solving		■		■	■	■	■		■	■	■	■	■	■	■	■	■	■	■	■	■	■			
Reasoning, Proof		■		■	■	■	■		■	■	■	■	■	■	■	■	■	■	■			■			
Communication							■			■	■				■						■				
Connections				■	■	■	■	■	■		■	■	■			■	■		■		■	■	■		
Representation												■							■						

NCTM Standard	26	27	28	29	30	31	32	33	34	35	36	37	38	39	40	41	42	43	44	45	46	47	48	49	50
Number, Operation	■	■	■	■	■	■	■	■	■	■	■	■	■	■	■	■	■	■	■	■	■	■	■	■	■
Algebra																			■	■			■		
Geometry						■												■							
Measurement						■																			
Data Analysis, Probability																									
Problem Solving						■	■	■	■	■	■	■	■	■	■	■	■	■	■	■	■	■	■	■	■
Reasoning, Proof						■	■	■	■	■	■	■	■	■	■	■	■	■	■	■	■	■	■	■	■
Communication									■								■							■	■
Connections	■					■								■						■					
Representation	■																								

NCTM Standard	51	52	53	54	55	56	57	58	59	60	61	62	63	64	65	66	67	68	69	70	71	72	73	74	75
Number, Operation	■	■	■	■	■	■	■	■	■	■	■	■	■	■			■		■	■		■			■
Algebra		■				■	■				■									■					
Geometry																					■	■			
Measurement															■	■	■	■	■	■	■	■	■		
Data Analysis, Probability																									
Problem Solving	■	■	■	■	■	■	■	■	■	■	■	■	■		■	■	■	■	■	■	■	■			■
Reasoning, Proof	■	■	■	■	■	■	■	■	■	■	■	■	■		■	■	■		■	■	■	■	■	■	■
Communication	■	■					■		■						■	■			■	■		■	■		
Connections				■		■					■			■		■	■		■	■	■	■		■	
Representation				■		■							■		■	■	■	■					■	■	■

ACTIVITIES ACCORDING TO
NATIONAL MATHEMATICS STANDARDS

NCTM Standard	76	77	78	79	80	81	82	83	84	85	86	87	88	89	90	91	92	93	94	95	96	97	98	99	100
Number, Operation		■	■	■	■	■	■	■	■	■								■						■	
Algebra															■								■	■	■
Geometry		■		■				■	■	■	■	■	■	■		■	■	■	■	■	■	■	■	■	■
Measurement	■			■																					
Data Analysis, Probability						■																			
Problem Solving	■	■	■	■	■	■		■	■	■	■	■	■	■	■	■	■	■	■	■	■	■	■	■	■
Reasoning, Proof	■	■	■	■	■	■		■	■	■	■	■	■	■	■	■	■	■	■	■	■	■	■	■	■
Communication	■					■								■	■			■				■			
Connections	■	■	■	■				■		■		■	■	■	■			■	■			■	■	■	
Representation	■							■						■								■			■

NCTM Standard	101	102	103	104	105	106	107	108	109	110	111	112	113	114	115	116	117	118	119	120	121	122	123	124	125	126
Number, Operation	■	■	■		■	■			■	■	■			■	■		■		■			■	■	■	■	■
Algebra					■		■																■	■		
Geometry				■																						
Measurement			■	■																						
Data Analysis, Probability																										
Problem Solving	■	■	■	■	■		■	■	■	■	■	■	■	■	■	■	■	■	■	■	■	■	■	■	■	■
Reasoning, Proof	■	■	■	■	■		■	■	■	■	■	■	■	■	■	■	■	■	■	■			■	■		■
Communication							■	■		■		■	■	■				■	■		■	■				■
Connections		■		■		■		■		■	■		■				■		■	■	■		■		■	
Representation		■	■									■	■					■				■		■		

PLACE VALUE AND MONEY

1. A caller gives a place value clue, such as, "I'm thinking of a number that has 6 hundreds, 3 tens, and 5 ones." The caller chooses another student to write the numeral on the board (635). If successful, the student doing the writing becomes the caller.

   Variation: Divide the class into teams by rows, etc. The teacher is the caller. Points determine the winning team.

   Variation: Use a different number of places.

2. This activity is for 1 to 4 players and requires a die numbered 0 to 5, base-ten blocks, score pad, or calculator. For each roll of the die, the player receives that number of unit cubes (ones). The first to build a ten (a ten is made up of 10 unit cubes) wins.

   Variation: Play to 20, 30, 40, etc.

   Variation: Use base-ten blocks with the following values: cube/unit, long/ten, flat/hundred. Follow the same strategy. Students could make trades of equal value to acquire blocks of different value. The goal would be to build a hundred first.

3. Each row contains one or more pairs of addends and their sum. Loop the addends and sum. The loops may overlap in a row. The order must be addends, then sum. An example has been done for you (1 + 2 = 3).

4. Have each student write the number of members of their family. Add 14. Subtract 7. Add 93. Have a student announce the answer. Remove the hundreds digit from the value given and the result is the number of people in that student's family.

5. Penny's parents had three kids. One was named Nickel, and one was named Dime. What was the name of their third kid?

6. The student picks two single-digit addends and the teacher picks three so that the sum of all five numbers is 26. Here's how:

For each number the student picks, the teacher chooses a number that pairs with it to sum to 9, the target number. (If the student picks 2 and 4, then the teacher picks 7 and 5 because 2 + 7 = 9 and 5 + 4 = 9.) Using 9 as the target number, the sum of the first four numbers will always be 18.

The fifth number (picked by the teacher) is called the "magic number." In this case, it's 8 because it's the number you add to the four others (which now total 18) to get a sum of 26.

You can vary the sum (of all five numbers) to be anything from 18 to 27, depending on your choice of the "magic number." If you pick zero as the magic number, the sum will be 18; pick 1 and the sum is 19, etc.; picking 9 as the magic number gives you a sum of 27.

Variation: Extend to use more addends. (Always an odd number, and the number of pairs determines the answer.)

Variation: Larger addends could be used. (Using five 3-digit addends would give a sum in the two thousands.)

7. The price of a ball and a glove is $32. If you get 2 balls and 3 gloves, the total price would be $86. What is the price of one ball?

Explain how you got your answer.

_____

_____

_____

8. Letters are assigned the values as listed. The task is to form words with either the greatest or least value by adding the worth of the letters in the word.

Points	Letters
1	A
2	E, L, O, T, N
5	B, I, R, S, U
10	C, D, G, H, M
20	F, P, V, W, Y
25	J, K, Q
30	X, Z

Variation: Multiply the value of the letters.

Variation: Use words from the current spelling list.

Variation: Use students' first or last names to see whose name is the most valuable.

9.   What does TTTT represent?

10.   How many counting numbers between 100 and 500 have at least one 2 in them?

Explain how you got your answer.

_____

_____

_____

11. If it costs 25 cents to make a straight cut on a board, how much will it cost to cut that board into 7 pieces?

Explain how you got your answer.

_____

_____

_____

12. Why are 1990 American dollar bills worth more than 1989 American dollar bills?

13. What number does TTTTTTT9 represent?

14. Arrange the digits 1 through 8 in the squares so that no digit is touching another that is one greater or less (for example, 3 cannot touch 2 or 4). A touch could be horizontal, vertical, or diagonal.

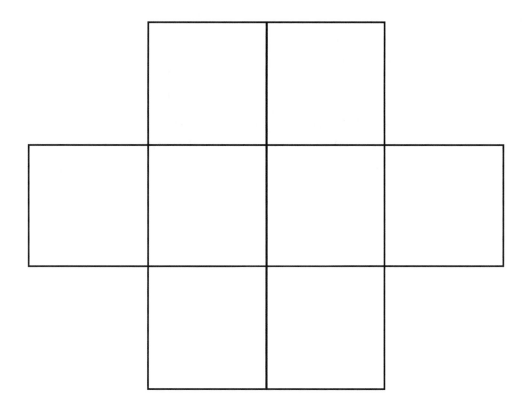

15. I am a 2-digit number less than 84. The sum of my digits is 9. The ones digit is twice the tens digit. Who am I?

Explain how you got your answer.

_____

_____

_____

16. Write any 3-digit number. Reverse the 3 digits. The ones digit of the original number becomes the hundreds digit of the new number. The hundreds digit of the original number becomes the ones digit of the new number. The tens digit will stay the same for both numbers. Add the original number and its reversal. If the sum can be read the same way both backwards and forwards, it is called a palindrome. If not, continue the process by reversing the digits of the sum and add it to the preceding sum. Continue until a palindrome appears.

17. Choose a 2-digit number with the tens digit greater than the ones digit. Reverse the number and subtract the new number from the original one. If you get a single digit answer, put a zero in the tens place, even though we do not usually do that. For example, if your subtraction answer is 7, write it as 07. Reverse the digits in the missing addend (subtraction answer) and add that value to the missing addend.

18. Choose any two-digit number. Multiply that two-digit number by 2. Add 5. Multiply that new sum by 50. Subtract 365 from that answer. Add any other two-digit number you pick to the answer you got when subtracting. Add 115 to this new sum. What do you get?

19. Arrange 4 pennies, 4 nickels, 4 dimes, and 4 quarters on the grid so each row, column, and diagonal has exactly one of each coin in it.

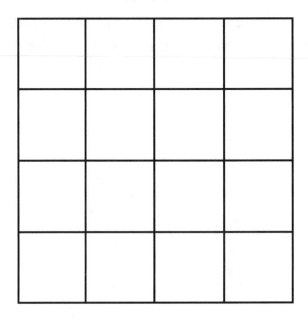

20. A number has 4 digits. None of the digits in the number are repeated. The digit in the thousands place is 3 times the digit in the tens place. The number is odd. The sum of the digits in the number is 27. What is the number?

Explain how you got your answer.

_____

_____

_____

21. A person bought a horse for $275, sold it for $295, bought it back for $325 and sold it again for $350. After all of that, has the person made or lost money, and how much?

Explain how you got your answer.

_____

_____

_____

22. If A is worth $0.01, B is worth $0.02, C is worth $0.03, etc., find a word worth $1.00 when adding the values of the letters in the word.

Variation: Find the value of students' first or last names.

Variation: Compare values for the greatest and least.

Variation: Let the letter value be in terms of dollars (A = $1, B = $2, etc.) and find a word worth $1,000,000 by multiplying the value of the letters.

23. If you were given the choice between taking 5000 dollars or 1 penny a day doubled each day for 20 days, which one would you choose?

Example: Day 1= $0.01, Day 2= $0.02, Day 3= $0.04, Day 4= $0.08...

Explain your answer.

_____

_____

_____

WHOLE NUMBER OPERATIONS

24. Form students into two facing lines. Give a bean bag to one student. That student states the operation part of a number fact (something like $3 + 4 =$) and tosses the bean bag to a person on the other team who must give the answer to the problem. A correct answer results in a point for the team. The team reaching a specified total is the winner. No student may be selected to answer more than 2 problems until all players have at least one opportunity.

25. You will need construction paper, markers, and glue for this activity. Each student receives or makes a paper headband. Display construction paper feathers so students can see them and have access to them. Write one basic fact on each feather. Students may take turns winning feathers for their headbands by accurately solving facts. When all feathers have been won, students may glue them to their headbands and wear their winnings. The student with the most feathers is "Chief of Facts" for the day. (See next page for feathers.)

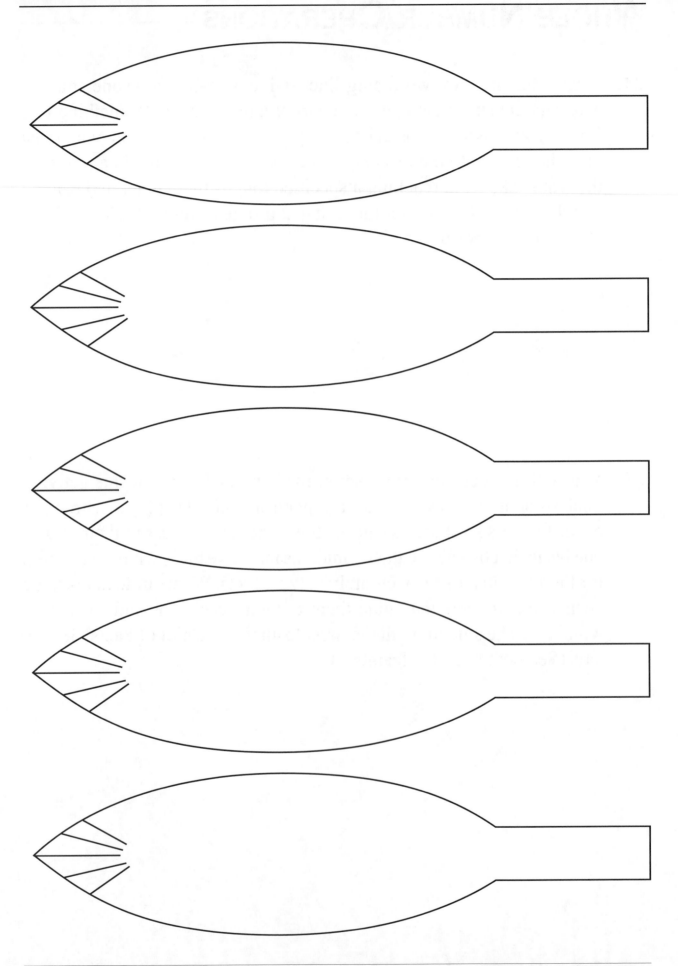

26. Use jump rope rhymes and bouncing balls for counting, skip counting, exercise, coordination, and fun for individuals, partners, groups, or the whole class.

Rhyme 1
I love stories and I love reading.
How many books will I be needing?
1, 2, 3, 4, … (or 2, 4, 6, 8, …)

Rhyme 2
Teacher, teacher!
Hear me count.
Will I reach the greatest amount?
5, 10, 15, 20, … (or some variation).

27. You will need cards, each with a number from zero through 9 and a set of cards with an addition (or subtraction, multiplication, or division) number fact written on them. The zero through 9 cards serve as "mailboxes." Read a number fact card and instruct a student to deliver that card to the correct mailbox. For example, the card that reads 3 + 4 would go to mailbox 7, so the student would put the card that reads 3 + 4 on top of the card that reads 7. Vary the values to suit the set of facts being used. (See the next three pages for card templates.)

1   2

3   4

5 6

7 8

9 10

28. Students respond only to statements prefaced with "Simon asks" or they are out of the game. For example, they would respond to "Simon asks what is 4 + 8?" but not to "4 + 8 = ?" (because Simon did not ask). Vary the game by inserting statements that require only an action, such as "Simon asks you to touch your head."

29. A set of cards numbered 1 through 10 is dealt to two players. The players decide who will be "even" and who will be "odd." Each player turns over one card. If the sum of the cards is odd, the "odd" player gets the cards. If the sum of the cards is even, the "even" player gets the cards. The game continues until one player is out of cards. See previous three pages for cards.

Variation: Find the difference of the values on the cards.

Variation: Find the product of the values on the cards.

30. Students stand one behind the other in front of the class. The teacher says, "Last person, stand on one foot." "The fourth student from the front, raise a hand." "The fifth person from the back, please clap your hands." "The third person from the front, return to your seat." Continue in this manner. Vary by adding players or changing commands.

31. Make a card for each student in the class or give one card to each pair of student partners. A sample set of cards follows on the next four pages. The first student reads a card statement. For example, "I have 15. Who has a number with a 4 in the tens place?" The game continues until a student reads a card that is answered with the first reader's card (15 in this case). Care should be taken to avoid duplicating the cards. If there are multiple answers, the first student answering correctly continues. Blanks are provided to make your own additions to the game.

I have 28. Who has a number with a 7 in the tens place and a 0 in the ones place?

I have 40. Who has a number with an 8 in the ones place?

I have 15. Who has a number with a 4 in the tens place?

I have 12. Who has a card with the number of sides of a triangle in the tens place and the number of sides of a square in the ones place?

I have 35. Who has a card whose numbers add up to 3?

I have 70. Who has a card with a 3 in the tens place and the number of fingers plus the thumb on one hand in the ones place?

I have 7. Who has the card with the number that is one less than 10?

I have 2. Who has the card that has the number of days in a week?

I have 34. Who has the card that tells the number of tens in 29?

I have 72. Who has the card with 1 ten and 5 ones?

I have 12. Who has the card that is one more than 71?

I have 9. Who has the card that tells how many things are in a dozen?

Use these blank cards to expand the activity. Cards can be copied and resized to fit on an index card.

32. Place a 1, 2, 3, 4, or 5 in each circle to get a sum of 8 on each side of the "V." No digit may be used more than once.

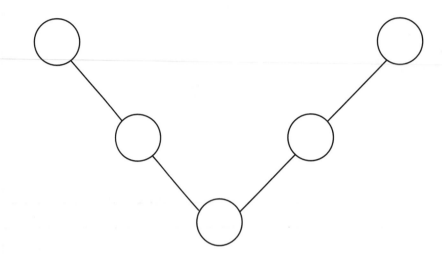

33. Put a 1, 2, 3, 4, or 5 in each circle to get a sum of 9 along each diagonal. No digit may be used more than once.

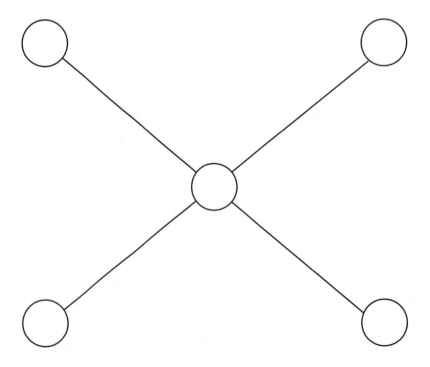

34. What number will come next?

2, 4, 6, _____

Explain how you got your answer.

_____

_____

_____

35. Use 1, 2, 3, 4, 5, 6, and 7 to fill the circles so that the sum of each row, column, or diagonal will be 12. Each digit may be used only once.

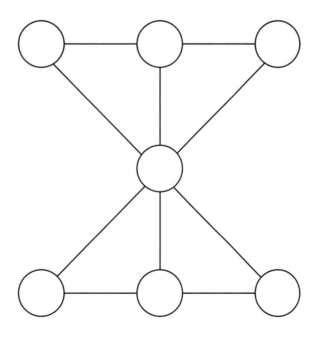

36. Use the digits 1 through 9 to fill in the cells so each horizontal, vertical, and diagonal row of three has a sum of 15. No digit may be used more than once.

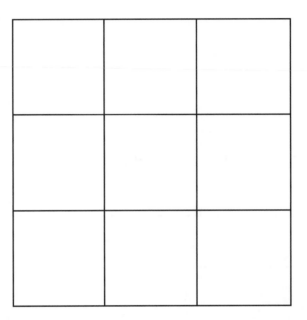

37. Work with a partner. Take turns calling out any number from 1 to 6, inclusive. As each number is called out, add it to the previous sum. The first player to reach 50 wins.

Variation: Enter the values into a calculator and pass it back and forth. The person receiving the calculator would see the 1 to 6 value entered by the other person. That person would then touch "+" before entering a new value and handing the calculator to the other player.

38. Work with a partner. One person picks a number from a point of a star. The other person tries to guess what it is. Ask which star or stars the number appears in. "Is it located in Star 1 or Star 3 or ...?" For example, if the number was in Star 1, Star 3, and Star 4, the secret number would be 8 because the sum of 1, 3, and 4 is 8.

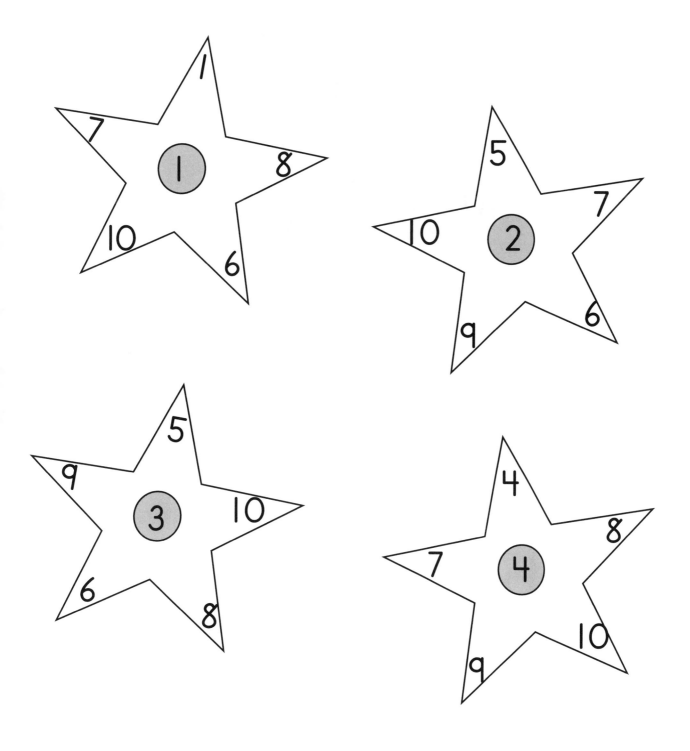

39. You are playing a Bean Bag Toss game in which you throw a bean bag onto a game board that has spaces worth the points shown. You have made 3 tosses, and your total for them is 101. Each time you tossed the bean bag, it landed on a different space. Where did the bean bag land on each of your 3 tosses?

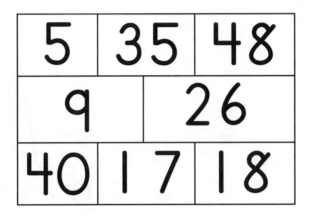

40. Write the next three numbers in this pattern:

1, 6, 3, 8, 5, 10, 7, ___, ___, ___

41. How can 7 be made even?

42. The product of three prime numbers less than 30 is 1,955. What are the numbers?

Explain how you got your answer.

_____

_____

_____

43. Add a line segment to make this statement true.

$$| + | = |0$$

44. Multiply your age by 3. Add 1. Multiply that answer by 3. Add your age. Cross off the ones digit of the answer and you will have your age.

45. Write a number. Add 6. Multiply this sum by 2. Subtract the original number. Subtract the original number again. Subtract 8. What did you get?

46. Given 9 8 7 6 5 4 3 2 1, where would you put plus signs so the values you create give a sum of 99? You may not change the order of the digits. One solution is $9 + 8 + 7 + 6 + 5 + 43 + 21 = 99$. What is another one?

47. How many times can you subtract the number 5 from the number 25 in the same problem?

48. Find the pattern in the following numbers and continue it by writing the next six numbers.

$$2, \ 7, \ 4, \ 8, \ 13, \ 10, \ 20, \ 25, \ 22, \ 44,$$

_____, _____, _____, _____, _____, _____

49. What are the next two terms in the sequence?

15   30   20   27   25   24   30   21   35   18 ___   ___

Explain how you got your answer.

_____

_____

_____

50. A little green frog is sitting at the bottom of the stairs. The frog wants to get to the tenth step, and leaps forward 2 steps and then back 1. Then the frog leaps another 2 steps forward and back 1. How many forward leaps will the frog have to take to get to the tenth step, if this same pattern is followed?

Explain how you got your answer.

_____

_____

_____

51. There are ten digits (0, 1, 2, 3, 4, 5, 6, 7, 8, and 9) in our base 10 number system. When you multiply all ten of those digits together, what is the product?

Explain how you got your answer.

_____

_____

_____

52. The same pattern is used to get the first and second number in each row of the table below. Complete the table by replacing A, B, C, and D with numbers that follow the pattern.

First	Second
3	5
9	23
4	8
6	A
7	B
C	11
D	2

Explain in writing how the missing numbers in this table are found.

_____

_____

_____

53. Use each of 1, 2, 3, 4, 5, 6, 7, 8, and 9 exactly one time in the spaces given to make a true statement. You must use all nine of the counting numbers given. None of the counting numbers given may be used more than once.

$$\underline{\quad}\ \underline{\quad}\ \underline{\quad}\ \text{x}\ \underline{\quad}\ \underline{\quad}\ =\ \underline{\quad}\ \underline{\quad}\ \underline{\quad}\ \underline{\quad}$$

54. Twin primes are found when the smaller of two prime numbers subtracted from the larger gives you the number 2. How many pairs of twin primes are there that are less than 100?

55. Write your age. Add 90 to it. Cross off the digit in the largest place value slot (tens or hundreds). Add the crossed-off digit to what is left after it is crossed off. Subtract 9 from this number (if you are 10 or older, add 9 rather than subtracting). What did you get?

56. Work with a partner. One student is to pick two numbers that are opposite each other on the clock (like 3 and 9). Say: "Add the two numbers but tell me only the sum. I'll tell you the addends you used to get the sum."

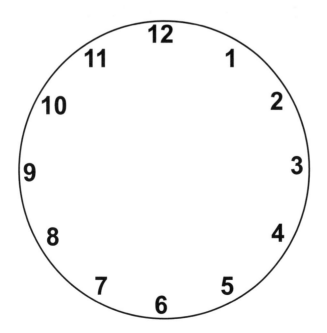

57. What is the 50th number in this sequence?

$$5, 11, 17, 23, 29, 35, 41, \ldots$$

Explain how you got your answer.

_____

_____

_____

58. Choose a number. Multiply it by 100. Subtract the original number. Add the digits. If that sum has more than one digit, add those digits together and continue doing that until you get a single digit answer. What did you get?

59.   What will come next?

20, 30, 40, 10, 12, 18, 24, 6, 35, 30, 25, _____

Explain how you got your answer.

_____

_____

_____

60.   For each letter, find the correct digit. Each letter stands for a different digit.

$$
\begin{array}{r}
\text{EFGH} \\
\times \quad 4 \\
\hline
\text{HGFE}
\end{array}
$$

61. Name the next value in the sequence below.

39, 13, 78, 87, 75, 25, 150, 159, 147, ___

62. Insert one pair of parentheses to make the following sentence true.

40 − 6 x 6 − 2 − 6 = 10

63. Students sit in a circle or semicircle. Count the number of students and divide this sum by two, to get the number of student pairs. Assign numbers from one to the number of student pairs, with each number being used twice. A student leader calls out an addition fact, such as 7 + 5 and the two students who were assigned 12 must exchange places before the leader can get to one of their places. If the leader succeeds, the student without a place becomes the new leader. The old leader is given that student's number. Proceed until all possible sums have been called. Remember not to choose an addition fact whose answer exceeds the number of student pairs.

64. Pick a number. Add 4. Subtract 3. Add 5. Subtract 3. Add 2. Subtract 5. What did you get?

65. Seven of the twelve months have 31 days in them. Eleven of the twelve months have 30 days in them. How many months have 28 days in them?

66. Before Mount Everest was discovered, what was the highest mountain on Earth?

67. An adult weighing 80 kilograms and 2 children, each weighing 40 kilograms, want to cross a river. Any of the 3 is able to row the one boat they have. The boat can hold only 80 kilograms on any one trip. How many trips will it take to get all 3 across a river? Remember that one trip is one time across the river, in either direction.

Explain how you got your answer.

_____

_____

_____

68. Which would be heavier—a pound of bricks or a pound of paper clips?

69. Two rabbits each weigh the same. There are two boxes that each weigh the same. If the total weight of the two rabbits and two boxes is 18 pounds, and the weight of one box is 3 pounds, what does one rabbit weigh?

Explain how you got your answer.

_____

_____

_____

70. Together, two dogs (Fido and Mydough) weigh 78 kilograms. Fido weighs twice as much as Mydough. How much does each dog weigh?

Explain how you got your answer.

_____

_____

_____

71. The squares shown are made up of 12 line segments. Move exactly 3 line segments to create exactly 4 squares, each of which is the same size as the ones shown.

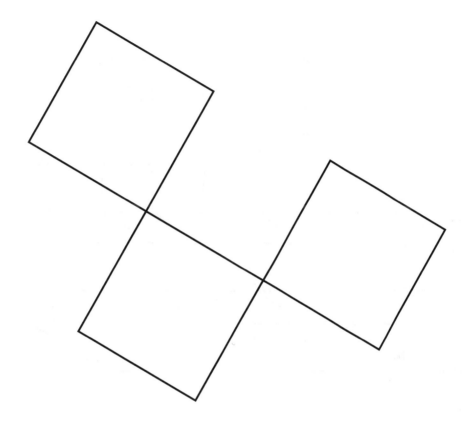

72. How many blocks does it take to make the set of steps shown? Assume the steps are not hollow.

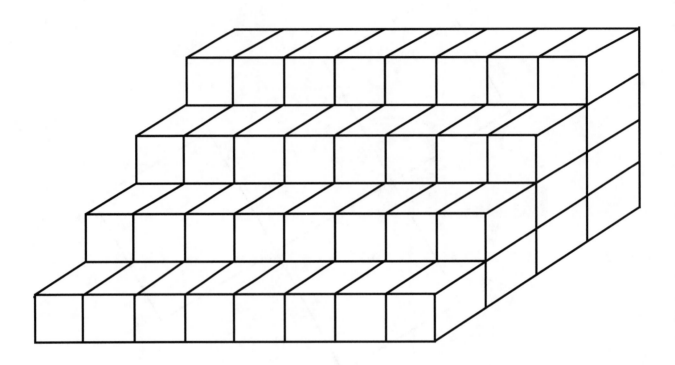

Explain how you got your answer.

_____

_____

_____

73. In what year did Christmas and New Year's fall in the same year?

Explain how you got your answer.

_____

_____

_____

74. How many cubic inches of dirt are there in a hole that is one foot deep, two feet wide, and six feet long?

Explain your answer.

_____

_____

75. A kid was born on December 27. The kid's birthday is always in the summer. How can that be?

76. Below is a picture of a broken watch. How can you tell that the watch is broken?

77. Player 1 thinks of a mathematical term or phrase and draws a blank line segment for each letter. Other players take turns guessing the missing letters. If the letter guessed is in the word, it is written on the appropriate blank. If the letter is not in the word, Player 1 draws a head on the gallows. Player 1 draws other body parts for each wrong guess (hat, head, neck, body, arms, legs, hands, feet). Player 2 wins if the word or phrase is completed before the hanging victim is completely drawn.

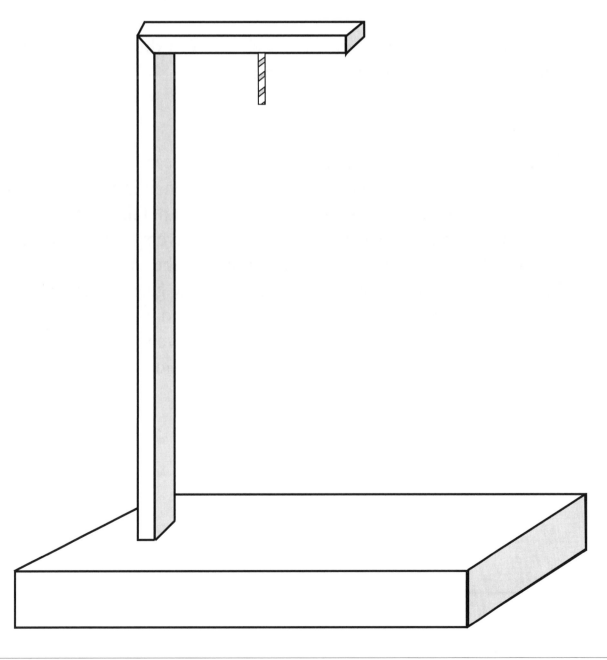

78. Roll one die to determine the number of digits in a target numeral. For example, a "3" would indicate that the target numeral will have 3 digits. In this example with 3 digits, the next roll will be the digit in the hundreds place. A third roll gives the digit in the tens place, etc. Partners take turns rolling. The winner has the number with the greater (or lesser) value.

Variation: The first roll determines the number of places for the target number. All other rolls may be used in whatever place the individual desires to gain the largest (or smallest) possible result. Once a value is placed, it may not be moved.

Variation: Use a pair of dice and use the tens digit of any roll as a substitute for a number in the next place.

79. You will need 36 cards for each game. Lay the cards face down, in a 6 by 6 array, on a flat surface. For younger children, it is helpful to outline the cards on poster board so they know where to put them. Perhaps with younger children, fewer cards could be used. Players take turns revealing 2 cards. If there is a match, the player removes the cards and continues. The player with the most cards at the end of the game wins. Suggested types of cards: number facts; geometry names and figures; base 10 block pictures and numerals; values rounded to a given precision; standard notation and expanded notation; digital and analog time; measurement units to be used with an object; etc.

80. How many different whole numbers can be made using at least one of the digits 2, 5, 8? The whole number may have 1, 2, or 3 digits in it but a digit may not be repeated within any one number. No digits other than 2, 5, and 8 may be used.

81. A black container has 3 red marbles and 2 blue ones in it. A gold container has 2 red marbles and 1 blue one in it. If you have to take a red marble out of one container to win a prize and you are not allowed to look in either container when you pick, which container gives you the best chance of winning the prize, the black one or the gold one?

Explain how you got your answer.

_____

_____

_____

82. You will need two cubes, each of which has faces numbered 1 through 6. Students may work in pairs or small groups. Each player writes the numbers 2 through 12 on a piece of paper. Player 1 tosses the cubes and crosses out the sum of the two numbers showing on the top of the cubes. This player will continue tossing, adding, and crossing out sums as long as a sum that appears on that player's paper can be eliminated. Duplication of a sum ends the game for that player. Continue play until all players have had a turn. The player with the most sums crossed out wins.

83. Make "giant" dominoes out of construction paper. (For overhead dominoes, use rectangles of construction paper with holes to resemble domino dot patterns.) Distribute the giant dominoes to students. Write a numeral on the board and ask students to stand if they have the domino with that sum.

Variation: Have students hold up the domino if they think they have a solution.

Variation: Students identify the dot sum that is one less or one more than the dot sum shown.

Variation: Have students place the overhead dominoes in order according to the sum of the dots—from least to greatest or from greatest to least.

Variation: Use the overhead dominoes to practice addition facts or to model families of related facts. For example, the domino shown has a total of 7 dots. One side has 3 dots and the other side has 4 dots. The sum is 7. Write the facts (2 addition facts and 2 subtraction facts) that can be generated using 3, 4, and 7. ($3 + 4 = 7$; $4 + 3 = 7$; $7 - 3 = 4$; $7 - 4 = 3$)

Variation: Find products instead of sums.

Variation: Express the dots from the two sides as a ratio, either greater than one, less than one, or equaling one.

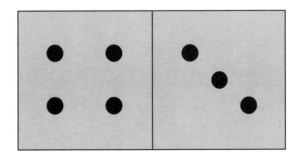

84. Place the digits 1, 2, 3, 4, 5, and 6 in the circles so that the sum of each side of the triangle is 10. A digit may not be used more than once.

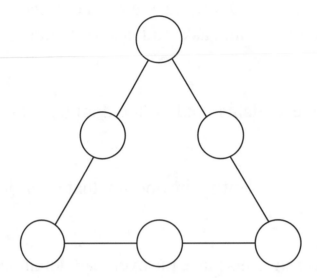

85. Use each digit 1 through 6 only once to fill in the diagram below. Write one digit in each circle so the sum of the digits on any side of the triangle is 9 AND ALSO so the sum of the two digits at the end of each of the line segments shown is also 9.

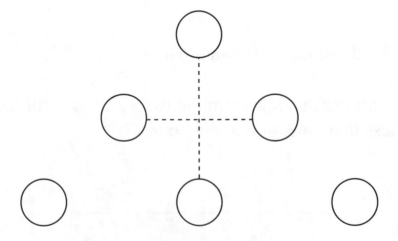

86. Count the circles in the drawing below.

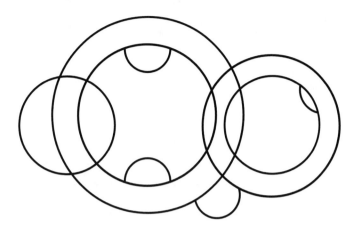

87. Count the triangles in the drawing below.

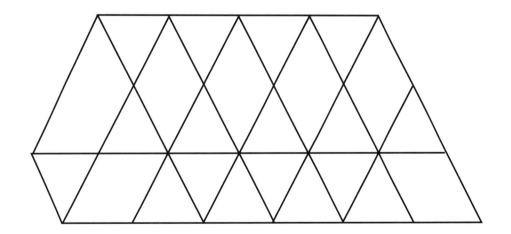

88. Work with a partner. One player will be "X" and the other, "O" Take turns marking Xs and Os in a square in the grid. The player that gets 5 in a row horizontally, vertically, or diagonally wins.

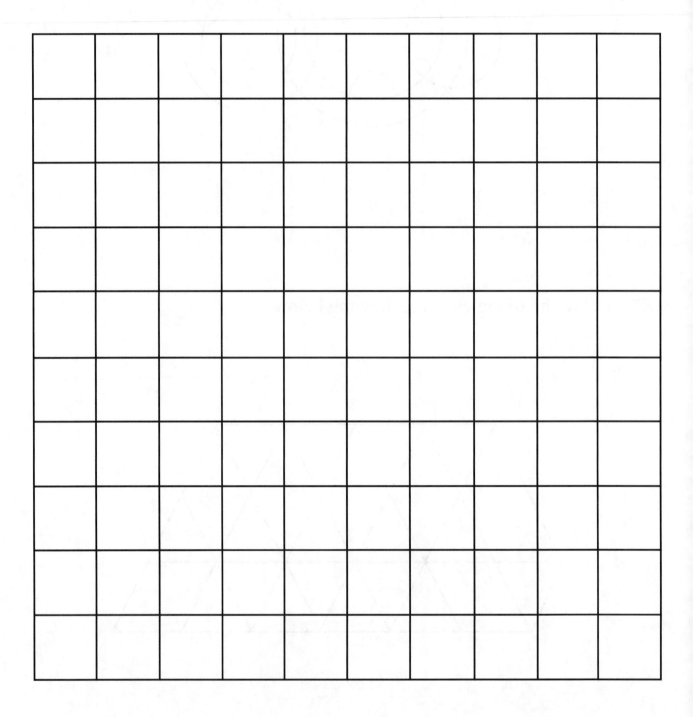

89. Four of the figures in the boxes below have something in common. List at least one box whose figure is different from the other four, then explain why. There are two correct answers.

 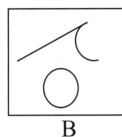 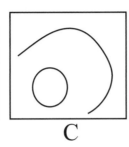 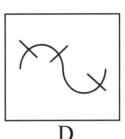 

A   B   C   D   E

_____

_____

_____

90. What will come next?

Antonio, Barbara, Chantel, Doreen, _____

Explain how you got your answer.

_____

_____

91. Each of a farmer's 3 movable chicken pens are in the shape of an equilateral triangle. The pens are all the same size, and each has the most chickens it can possibly hold. How can the pens be moved to make another equilateral triangle pen that is the same size as the original 3 to hold some new chickens the farmer obtains?

92. Count the squares in the drawing below.

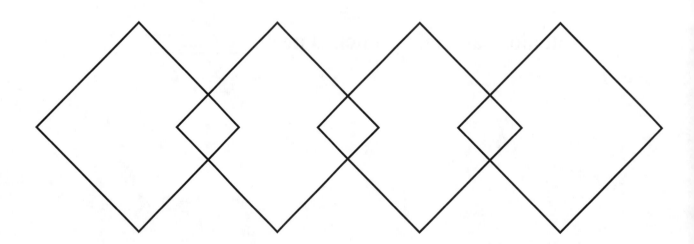

93. How many squares can you count in a 4 x 4 checkerboard?

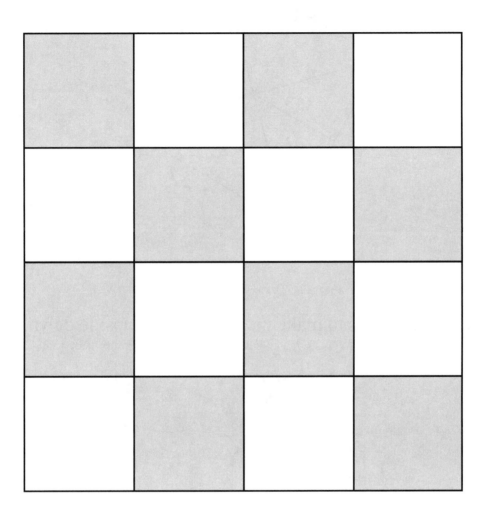

Explain how you got your answer.

_____

_____

_____

94.   Count the squares and triangles in the drawing below.

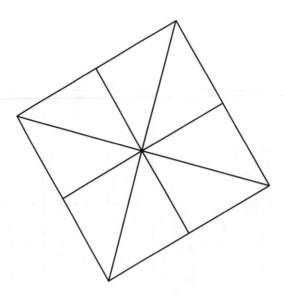

95.   Move exactly 3 X's to make the triangle turn upside down.

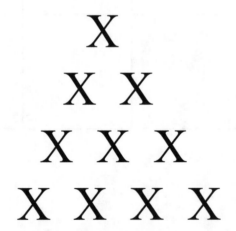

96. Draw or trace the shape below without lifting your pencil and without retracing any segments. (It is OK to cross a segment or pass through a point more than once.)

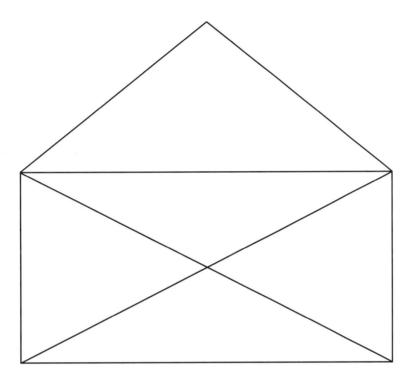

97.   Where should the Z be placed and why?

A		E F	H I	K L M N		T	V W X Y
	B C D	G	J		O P Q R S	U	

98.   Stamps can be purchased in large sheets where the stamps can be torn apart at the places where they touch each other. How many different ways can you buy 4 attached square stamps? Two ways are considered the same if one way can be turned or flipped so that its outline looks like another one. Use X's or little squares to show the ways you get your answer.

99. How many rectangles are in the figure below?

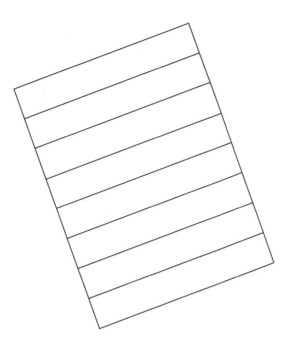

100. The letters in each of the following rows have some common special characteristic. (We are not talking about them being letters of the alphabet or the number of letters in a row. There could be other letters in each row, but you should have enough to make a decision.) Describe that characteristic for each row.

Row 1:   A, H, M, O, T, U, V, W, X, Y
Row 2:   B, C, D, H, I, O, X
Row 3:   H, O, X

FRACTIONS AND DECIMALS

101. Use each of the digits 1, 2, 4, and 8 once to make a number sentence that equals zero. You may use any operation (add, subtract, multiply, or divide) as many times as you wish. You may use parentheses in your solution.

102. Show that 6 is half of 11.

103. Twenty-five elementary school kids are going on a field trip in rented vans. Each rented van has seven seat belts. Each traveler must occupy a seat-belted seat. How many vans are needed for the field trip?

104. Look at the picture below. Suppose all the dots are one foot apart. If the dots were connected, all the created small squares would be the same size. What is the area of the inside of the goofy figure (the shaded part in the picture)?

Explain how you got your answer.

_____

_____

_____

105. A half is a third of it. What is it?

106. A leader writes a mystery number between 1 and 100. Volunteers take turns guessing the number. If a guess is greater than the mystery number, the leader raises both arms. If the guessed number is less that the mystery number, the leader squats. The student who identifies the mystery number becomes the leader.

Patterns and Problem Solving

107. What will come next?

X O X X O O X X X

Explain how you got your answer.

_____

_____

_____

108. What animal will come next?

dog, bird, tiger, kitten, _____

Explain how you got your answer.

_____

_____

_____

109. Complete the following figure by replacing each X with an odd counting number from 1 through 31 so there is a pattern in the table. Each odd counting number may appear only once in the final table.

X	17	X	1
29	X	13	X
X	21	X	5
25	X	9	7

110. Suppose that as you walk to school, you count 14 trees on the right side of the street. Later, when you walk home following the same route, you count 14 trees on the left side of the street. How many different trees did you count in all?

Explain how you got your answer.

_____

_____

_____

111. You have several single socks in your drawer. They are all the same style, but 9 of them are red and 8 of them are blue. If you cannot see the colors, what is the smallest number of socks you have to take from the drawer so you are sure to have a pair that is the same color?

Explain how you got your answer.

_____

_____

_____

112. What will come next?

rose, car, daisy, carrot, pansy, horse, _____

Explain how you got your answer.

_____

_____

_____

113. What comes next?

apples, beans, corn, _____

Explain how you got your answer.

_____

_____

_____

114. What animal would be the next one in this list?

dog, crow, tiger, osprey, _____

Explain how you got your answer.

_____

_____

115. Change the letters around in "eleven plus two" to get an equivalent statement. All letters must be used and no extra letters are permitted. That is, you are to use all 13 letters from "eleven plus two"; no more, no less.

116. Remove ten letters from the ones below to make an important word.

ITMEPNORLETTTANTWOERRDS

117. What is the next letter in the sequence:

$$O, T, F, S, N, E, \underline{\hphantom{XXXX}}$$

118. This problem might seem odd to you, but it really is not. Where should 9 and 10 be placed—above or below the segment, and why?

```
    1   2   3           6   7   8
 _____
 0               4   5
```

Explain how you got your answer.

_____

_____

119. You are given 5 beans and 4 bowls. Using all the beans, place an odd number of beans in each bowl.

Explain how you got your answer.

_____

_____

_____

_____

_____

120. Secretly assign each student in a group one of the following animal names: snake, spider, centipede, penguin, zebra, butterfly, etc. The other students are to guess each student's animal by asking questions. Players are not permitted to ask, "What animal are you?"

121. There are 9 stalls in a barn. Each stall will hold only 1 horse. If there are 10 horses and only 9 stalls, how can all the horses fit into the 9 stalls without placing more than one horse in each stall?

Explain how you got your answer.

_____

_____

_____

122. Here are several pairs of numbers that can be used to figure out what number should replace the question mark in the last pair. What number should replace the question mark?

$$(1, 3); \ (2, 3); \ (3, 5); \ (4, 4); \ (5, 4);$$
$$(6, 3); \ (7, 5); \ (8, 5); \ (9, 4); \ (10, ?)$$

Explain how you got your answer.

_____

_____

_____

123. What is the missing number in this puzzle?

P7 H4 O6 N6 E__

124. Explain what is unusual about the following sentence.

"I do not know every plane's precise location."

_____

_____

_____

125. When you spell the names of the counting numbers (one, two, three, . . .), what is the first one that will contain the letter "a"?

126. What is the next number in this sequence and why?

$$10, \quad 4, \quad 3, \quad 11, \quad 15, \quad \underline{\hspace{1.5cm}}$$

A. 14   **C.** 17

B. 1   **D.** 12

Explain how you got your answer.

_____

_____

_____

SOLUTIONS

1. Varies

2. Varies

3.

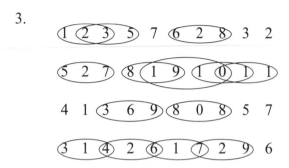

4. Varies

5. Penny is the third kid. "Penny's parents" is the clue. Many students will make up names for the third child since only Nickel and Dime seem to be named.

6. Varies. In the example below, the student choices are 2 and 4, making the teacher choices 7 and 5, respectively. That leaves 8 to be the magic number, since $26 - 2 - 4 - 7 - 5 = 8$.

   8 magic number

   7 teacher choice

   5 teacher choice

   4 student choice

   2 student choice

   } sum of 9

7. Ball = 10 and Glove = 22. You know that 1 ball + 1 glove together cost $32. Multiply that $32 by 2 and you know that 2 balls & 2 gloves cost $64. If you subtract the cost of 2 balls & 2 gloves ($64) from the cost of 2 balls & 3 gloves ($86) the answer is the cost of 1 glove ($22). Subtract the cost of one glove ($22) from the cost of 1 ball

& 1 Glove ($32) to get the cost of one ball ($10).

OR

Let X = ball and Y = glove

(1) X + Y = 32

(2) 2X + 3Y = 86

(3) 2X + 2Y = 64

Subtract (2) from (3) and get Y = 22, making X = 10.

Checking, 2(10) + 3(22) = 20 + 66 = 86

Note: Elementary students probably would not use X and Y, but that type thinking could occur and is a critical foundation for the study of algebra. This particular problem is a wonderful example of multistep problems that frequently prove challenging for students.

8. Varies

9. Four Ts = forty. This idea of having letters represent something is a formative part of the algebraic background you are building with your students. This helps them become accustomed to viewing letters in a nontypical context.

10. 157. There are 100 numbers from 200 to 299. Each one of them has at least one 2 in it. There are 30 more numbers with a 2 in the ones place (112, 352, etc.). The numbers between 200 and 299 inclusive are excluded because they have already been counted. There are 30 more numbers with a 2 in the tens place (125, 328, 427, etc.). Again, the numbers between 200 and 299 inclusive are excluded. But 122, 322, and 422 are counted twice in that process. Therefore, there are $100 + 30 + 30 - 3 = 157$ counting

numbers with a 2 in them between 100 and 500.

Rubric: 6 possible points

1 point (content): Recognition of the 100 numbers with a 2 in them between 200 and 299 inclusive

1 point (content): Recognition of the 30 numbers with a 2 in the ones place

1 point (content): Recognition of the 30 numbers with a 2 in the tens place

1 point (content): Recognition of the double counting in 122, 322, and 422

1 point (content): Correct arithmetic to get the total of 157

1 point (clarity): Explanation clearly written.

11. $1.50 or $0.75. 7 pieces means 6 cuts. 6($0.25) = $1.50

OR

Cut one piece into two parts. Place one piece on top of the other and make a second cut, giving 4 pieces. Stack 3 of those 4 pieces and make a third cut, giving a total of 7 pieces when the 1 that had not been cut is considered.

Rubric: 3 possible points

1 point (content): Correct number of cuts as either 6 cuts or 3 cuts

1 point (content): Correct arithmetic of cost as either $1.50 or $0.75

1 point (clarity): Explanation clearly written.

12. One thousand nine hundred ninety dollar bills are worth one dollar more than one thousand nine hundred eighty-nine dollar bills.

13. 79. The seven Ts can be pronounced 70. Presenting students with questions such as this can be an asset as they begin their study of basic algebra.

14. Answer could vary. See graphic below:

15. 36. Since you have a 2-digit number, and one digit is twice the other, the smaller digit must be 1, 2, 3, or 4 so the possible beginning answers are 12, 24, 36, 48, 21, 42, 63, and 84. Since the number is less than 84, the answer cannot be 84. That leaves candidates of 12, 24, 36, 48, 21, 42, and 63. Since the ones digit is twice the tens digit, you have 12, 24, and 36. Since the sum of the digits in the answer is 9, the answer must be 36.

Rubric: 4 possible points

1 point (content): Using 12, 24, 36, 48, 21, 42, 63, and 84 from one digit being twice the other

1 point (content): Using 36 or 63 because the sum of the digits is 9

1 point (content): Using 36 because the ones digit is twice the tens digit

1 point (clarity): Explanation clearly written

16. Varies. Examples:

$213 + 312 = 525$

$762 + 267 = 1029$

$1029 + 9201 = 10230$

$10230 + 03201 = 13431$

17. 99. Examples:

$$\begin{array}{r} 54 \\ -\ 45 \\ \hline 09 \\ +\ 90 \\ \hline 99 \end{array} \qquad \begin{array}{r} 73 \\ -\ 37 \\ \hline 36 \\ +\ 63 \\ \hline 99 \end{array}$$

18. The thousands and hundreds digits will make up the first picked number. Tens and ones digits will make up the second picked number. Example:

Let F be the first number picked

F   27

2F   54

2F + 5   59

$50(2F + 5) = 100F + 250$ 2950

$(100F + 250) - 365 = 100F - 11$ 2585

Let S be the second number picked

S   63

$(100F - 115) + S$ 2648

$100F + S - 115 + 115 = 100F + S$ 2763

Note: Your students will not use algebra to solve this problem, but the skills involved here are critical background work for

algebra. This type of multistep problem is traditionally difficult for children.

19. This solution is not unique.

P	N	D	Q
Q	D	N	P
N	P	Q	D
D	Q	P	N

20. 9837. Since the thousands digit is 3 times the tens digit, the tens digit must be 3 at most but it could be 1, or 2 also. However, since the sum of the 4 digits is 27, the thousands digit needs to be large. So, start with the tens digit as a 3 and then the thousands digit is 9. That uses 12 of the allowed sum of 27. Since the number is odd, 7 is the largest value that can be used in the ones place. Now 19 of the total of 27 have been used. That leaves 8 for the hundreds digit and all requirements of the problem have been met.

Rubric: 4 possible points

1 point (content): Use of the logic that the thousands digit needs to be large

1 point (content): Arithmetic is correct when subtracting 12 from 27

1 point (content): Arithmetic is correct when subtracting 19 from 27

1 point (clarity): Explanation clearly written

21. $45. Think of the situation as if two different horses were involved. The person paid $275 for the first horse and sold it for $295, making $20. Then the person paid $325

for the second horse and sold it for $350, making $25. $20 + $25 = $45.

OR

The person paid $600 (275 + 325) and got $645 (295 + 350). 645 − 600 = 45.

Rubric: 3 possible points

1 point (content): Pattern of paying out and receiving more money each time

1 point (content): Correct arithmetic

1 point (clarity): Explanation clearly written

22. Possible answers: Turkey, lightning, telephone, highways, nosebleeds, elephants, contented, settles, imported, mittens, useless, squares, percents, clockwise, quadrangle

23. The answer that provides the most money is a penny a day for 20 days. Under this scenario, you would receive $5242.88 on the 20th day alone and have more than $10,000 for all 20 days combined. Start with the first penny. Double it to get 2 cents. Double that 2 cents to get 4 cents. Double that 4 cents to get 8 cents, etc., until you reach 20 doublings.

Day 1 = $0.01
Day 2 = $0.02
Day 3 = $0.04
Day 4 = $0.08
Day 5 = $0.16
Day 6 = $0.32
Day 7 = $0.64
Day 8 = $1.28
Day 9 = $2.56
Day 10 = $5.12
Day 11 = $10.24
Day 12 = $20.48
Day 13 = $40.96

Day 14 = $81.92
Day 15 = $163.84
Day 16 = $327.68
Day 17 = $655.36
Day 18 = $1310.72
Day 19 = $2621.44
Day 20 = $5242.88.

(Total = $10485.75—gotten by adding all 20 daily values)

The amount for the first day is 1 cent, which can be shown as $2^0 = 1$ (the exponent for the first day is the day number minus 1 or $2^{1-1} = 2^0 = 1$). The amount for the second day is 2 cents, which can be shown as $2^1 = 2$ (the exponent for the second day is the day number minus 1 or $2^{2-1} = 2^1 = 2$). The amount for the third day is 4 cents, which can be shown as $2^2 = 4$ (the exponent for the third day is the day number minus 1 or $2^{3-1} = 2^2 = 4$). Etc. The twentieth day would be $2^{20-1} = 2^{19} = 524288$ cents ($5242.88). The total for all twenty days would be 2^{20} cents minus 1 cent or 1,048,576 cents − 1 cent = 1,048,575 cents, which is $10,485.75.

Rubric: 3 possible points

1 point (content): Recognize the doubling pattern

1 point (content): Correct arithmetic

1 point (clarity): Explanation clearly written

Note: This problem is found in many locations and forms in the study of mathematics. It is consistently popular with students. It can be done with a calculator or by hand without the use of exponents, or with exponents (not likely for lower grade elementary students, but something you might want to experiment with).

24. Varies

25.   Varies

26.   Varies

27.   Varies

28.   Varies

29.   Varies

30.   Varies

31.   Varies

32.

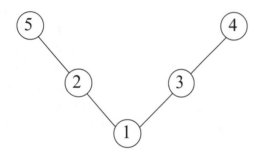

33.

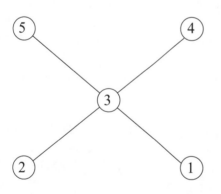

34.   8. Skip counting by 2 or adding 2 to the number before.

Rubric: 2 possible points

1 point (content): Recognize pattern

1 point (clarity): Explanation clearly written

35.   Note: 35 and 36 can be flipped vertically to provide an answer equally correct.

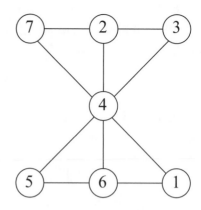

36.

2	9	4
7	5	3
6	1	8

37.   Varies. There is a strategy to this game. If 50 is the desired sum and you call a value that gives a sum of 43, you have lost the game. When you call 1 the sum is 44 and I call 6, giving 50. When you call 2 the sum is 45 and I call 5, giving 50. When you call 3 the sum is 46 and I call 4, giving 50. When you call 4 the sum is 47 and I call 3, giving 50. When you call 5 the sum is 48 and I call 2, giving 50. When you call 6 the sum is 49 and I call 1, giving 50. I can guarantee you get a sum of 43 by selecting a value that gives you a sum of 36. The logic would be the same as above except 50 would be replaced with 43 in each statement. Similarly, I can guarantee 36 with 29; 29 with 22; 22 with 15; 15 with 8; and 8 with 1. I lock into that sequence whenever necessary to guarantee my win. I will delay locking into that sequence to hide the pattern from you. The guaranteed initial number can be determined by dividing 50 by 7 (1 + 6 or the smallest permitted selection plus the largest permitted selection) and looking at the remainder. Vary the values that can be added or the sum to build toward the

generalization that will work in all cases.

38. Varies

39. 26, 35, 40. By enlarging the board, the idea could be used to make a game for the classroom, which would provide addition and subtraction of whole numbers practice. Students could use data gathered from the playing of the game to create problems—similar to the one given—that other students could solve.

40. 12, 9, 14. Add 5, subtract 3, add 5, subtract 3, etc. This pattern also has two separate versions of add 2: A, B, A + 2, B + 2, A + 4, B + 4, A + 6, B + 6, etc.

41. Take away the "s" in the spelling of "seven." Other answers that could be considered correct: add any odd number; multiply by any even number; subtract 1; add 1; etc. Note: It is important for students to realize that there is not always just one right answer in mathematics. This problem can help stimulate divergent thinking.

42. 5, 17, and 23. The different primes could be tested. The smallest one, 5, should be identified quickly because of the ability to divide any number ending in 5 by 5.

Rubric: 3 possible points

1 point (content): Recognition of divisibility by 5 in explanation

1 point (content): Arithmetic correct

1 point (clarity): Explanation clearly written

43. $1 + 1 \neq 10$

44. Varies. Examples:

Let A be your age	9	12
3A	27	36
3A + 1	28	37
3(3A + 1) = 9A + 3	84	111
9A + 3 + A = 10A + 3	93	123

Cross off the 3 (ones)   9   12

Your students will not use algebra to solve this problem, but they are learning important skills that form the foundations of algebra. They tradionally find this type of multistep problem difficult.

45. Examples:

Let A be your number	7	15
P + 6	13	21
2(P + 6) = 2P + 12	26	42
(2P + 12) − P = P + 12	19	27
(P + 12) − P = 12	12	12
12 − 8 = 4	4	4

Your students will not use algebra to solve this problem, but they are learning important skills that form the foundations of algebra. They tradionally find this type of multistep problem difficult.

46. $9 + 8 + 7 + 65 + 4 + 3 + 2 + 1 = 99$

This solution is mostly guess and check. It can be done by hand or with technology. Some students might notice the need to have at least one odd addend since the sum is odd.

47. Once. After you do the first subtraction, you would be subtracting from 20.

48. 49, 46, 92, 97, 94, 188. Add 5, subtract 3, multiply by 2, repeat.

X

X + 5

X + 5 − 3 = X + 2

2(X + 2)

Your students will not use the algebra shown

here to do the problem, but the idea of connecting operations like this is essential background work for algebra.

49. 40 and 15. There are two sequences in one. The first one is the odd numbered terms—15, 20, 25, 30, 35, 40—increasing by 5 each time. That is, 5 is added to every other term through the sequence, starting with 15. Skip a term, then add 5 to that initial 15 to get 20, the third term in the sequence. Skip a term and then add 5 to 20 to get the fifth term in the sequence.

The second one is in the even numbered places—30, 27, 24, 21, 18, 15—decreasing by 3 each time. That is, 3 is subtracted from each even term, starting with the second term of 30. So the next even term is the fourth term, which is $30 - 3$ or 27. The next even term is the sixth term, which is $27 - 3$ or 24.

Rubric: 3 possible points

1 point (content): Recognition of the increasing pattern

1 point (content): Recognition of the decreasing pattern

1 point (clarity): Explanation clearly written

50. 9 forward leaps. Sample: up to 2, back to 1; up to 3, back to 2; up to 4, back to 3; up to 5, back to 4; up to 6, back to 5; up to 7, back to 6; up to 8, back to 7; up to 9, back to 8; up to 10 and FINISHED.

Rubric: 3 possible points

1 point (content): Pattern of 2 forward and 1 back

1 point (content): Correct counting and arithmetic

1 point (clarity): Explanation clearly written

51. 0. Since zero is one of the factors, the product is zero because zero times any number is zero.

OR

$0 \times 1 \times 2 \times 3 \times 4 \times 5 \times 6 \times 7 \times 8 \times 9 = 0$

Rubric: 2 possible points

1 point (content): Product of zero.

1 point (clarity): Explanation clearly written.

52. $A = 14$; $B = 17$; $C = 5$; $D = 2$.

Multiply the number in the first column by 3 and then subtract 4. To find the number in the first column, add 4 to the value in the second column and divide that answer by 3.

Note: Although your students probably will not be able to state a formula, you might recognize some basic algebra in their answers. The formula is Second column = 3 times First column minus 4.

Rubric: 3 possible points

1 point (content): Recognition of the pattern in the explanation

1 point (content): Table completed correctly

1 point (clarity): Explanation clearly written

53. $138 \times 42 = 5796$

$157 \times 28 = 4396$

$186 \times 39 = 7254$

198 x 27 = 5346

483 x 12 = 5796

297 x 18 = 5346

159 x 48 = 7632

Guess and check is going to be the dominant routine used here. Some number theory might be evident through rationalizations that if the ones digit in each factor is 8 and 9, the ones digit of the product must be 2 since 8 x 9 = 72. Encourage this type of thinking.

54. 8. Examples: 3&5, 5&7, 11&13, 17&19, 29&31, 41&43, 59&61, 71&73.

Note: This is a good problem for practice of divisibility rules or to introduce the Sieve of Eratosthenes (found in many textbooks.)

55. Your age. Examples:

Let A = your age (less than 10)

A   7

A + 90   7 + 90 = 97

Take away the 9 (A + 0)   7 + 0

Add 9 (A + 9)   7 + 9 = 16

Subtract 9 from this answer   16 – 9

(A + 9) – 9 = A   16 – 9 = 7

Let A = your age (more than 10)

A   60

A + 90   60 + 90 = 150

Take away the 1   50

Add 1 (A – 9)   60 – 9 = 51

Add 9 to this answer   51 + 9

(A – 9) + 9 = A   51 + 9 = 60

Note: Your students will probably not use the algebraic approach to solve this problem because they do not have those skills. However, the thought process involved is the same, even without the variable. Doing problems like this is a critical first step toward developing those necessary algebra skills. This is also a good example of a multistep problem that students need to become efficient at solving.

56. Divide the sum given by 2 and subtract 3 from that answer. That process will give you the smaller of the two numbers used. Add 6 to that number to get the larger of the two numbers used.

OR

Algebraically, let N = the smaller number. Then N + 6 is the larger.

N + (N + 6) = Sum

2N + 6 = Sum

2N = Sum – 6, the smaller number.

Note: Your students will probably not use the algebraic approach to solve this problem. However, the thought process involved is the same, even without the variable. Doing problems like this is a critical first step toward developing those necessary algebra skills. This is also a good example of a multistep problem that students need to become efficient at solving.

57. 299. The pattern involves a difference of 6 between adjacent terms of the sequence. Add 6 to 5, getting 11, then add 6 to 11 getting 17, then add 6 to 17 getting 23, etc., until 6 has been added 50 times, ending in 299. Although your students will not have this skill, the problem could be solved algebraically with 6N–1 where N stands for

number of terms. In this case, it would be 6 x 50 – 1 = 300 – 1 = 299. It is possible that some of the students will begin to see the possibility of approaching this type problem with a formula such as this.

Rubric: 3 possible points

1 point (content): Idea of adding six 50 times and getting 299

1 point (content): Idea of adding six but not doing it 50 times

1 point (clarity): Explanation clearly written

58. 9. Examples:

Pick 47

4700   Multiply by 100

4700 – 47 = 4653   Subtract 47

4+6+5+3 = 18   Add digits of answer

1+8=9   Add digits of answer

Pick 568

56800   Multiply by 100

56800 – 568 = 56232   Subtract 568

5+6+2+3+2=18 Add digits of answer

1+8=9   Add digits of answer

Pick 47921

4792100

4792100 – 47921 = 4744179

4+7+4+4+1+7+9 = 36

3+6=9

Note: Students may not select such large numbers but they should be encouraged

to work a variety of problems to create the suspicion that the answer is always 9. This suspicion becomes a foundation for the need to prove things.

59. 5. 5 is the largest common factor (5 is the largest number that divides into 35, 30, and 25 with a remainder of zero each time) of 35, 30, and 25, just as 6 is the largest common factor of 12, 18, and 24, and 10 is the largest common factor of 20, 30, and 40.

Rubric: 3 possible points

1 point (content): Recognition of the pattern of 3 multiples followed by their largest common factor

1 point (content): Recognition of the need for the greatest common factor

1 point (clarity): The explanation is clearly written

60. E = 2, F = 1, G = 7, H = 8. Since the product is 4 digits, E has to be 1 or 2 because 4 times anything else would mean there would have to be a digit in the ten thousands place. H cannot be 1 because there is no digit that can be multiplied by 4 to give 1. That means E must be 2, which forces H to be 8. The rest is guess and check.

61. 49. Starting with 39, you divide by 3, multiply that answer by 6, add 9 to that answer, and subtract 12 from that answer. The cycle is repeated.
Note: Notice the 3, 6, 9, 12 sequence within the operations.

62. See example below:
$$40 – 6 \times (6 – 2) – 6 = 40 – 6 \times (4) – 6$$
$$= 40 – 24 – 6$$
$$= 16 – 6$$
$$= 10$$

63. Varies

64. Varies. The additions and subtractions all add up to be 0, so students will end up with 0 + the number they chose. Example:

Pick a number	X	4
Add 4	X + 4	8
Subtract 3	(X + 4) − 3 = X + 1	5
Add 5	(X + 1) + 5 = X + 6	10
Subtract 3	(X + 6) − 3 = X + 3	7
Add 2	(X + 3) + 2 = X + 5	9
Subtract 5.	(X + 5) − 5 = X	4

Note: Your students will probably not use the algebraic approach to solve this problem because they do not have those skills. Doing problems like this is a critical first step toward developing those necessary algebra skills. This is also a good example of a multistep problem that students need to become efficient at solving.

65. All 12 months have 28 days in them. This problem can cause an interesting discussion about whether we mean 28 or more (giving the answer of all) or   exactly 28 (giving the answer of one) when we say 28 days. Responding with an answer different from the majority provides an opportunity for discussion.

66. Mount Everest—it just hadn't been discovered.

67. 5. (Trip 1) 2 kids cross. (Trip 2) 1 kid returns. (Trip 3) Adult crosses. (Trip 4) Kid returns. (Trip 5) 2 kids cross.

Rubric: 3 possible points

1 point (content): Recognition of pattern needed to go back and forth

1 point (content): Minimum number of trips taken

1 point (clarity): Explanation clearly written

68. They weigh the same—one pound.

69. 6. 18 − 3 − 3 = 12, the weight of the rabbits.

Half of 12 is 6, the weight of one rabbit.

Rubric: 3 possible points

1 point (content): Recognition of the need to subtract the weight of 2 boxes from the total of 18 pounds

1 point (content): Recognition of the need to divide 12 by 2 for rabbit's weight

1 point (clarity): Explanation clearly written

70. Fido weighs 52 kg; Mydough weighs 26 kg. This solution is mostly guess and check. If students use algebra, they will probably define X as the weight of Mydough and say Fido's weight is 2X.

$$X + 2X = 78$$
$$3X = 78$$
$$X = 26$$

71. The dashed line segments are moved to the locations indicated by the thin line segments.

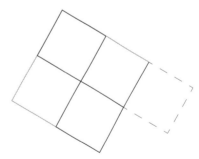

72. 80. The bottom layer will have 8 x 4 = 32 blocks, the next layer up will have 8 x 3 = 24 blocks, the next layer up will have 8 x 2 = 16 blocks, and the top layer will have 8 x 1 = 8 blocks for a grand total of 32 + 24 + 16 + 8 = 80.

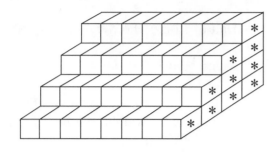

OR

Viewing the figure from the side, each left-to-right section (such as the one marked with asterisks in the graphic above) takes 10 blocks and there are 8 sections for a total of 80.

Rubric: 3 possible points

1 point (content): Recognition of at least one of the patterns

1 point (content): Correct arithmetic

1 point (clarity): Explanation clearly written

73. They fall in the same year every year. New Year's Day begins the year and Christmas arrives late the same year.

74. None. It is a hole. If you wanted to know how many cubic inches of dirt had been taken out of the hole, 1 ft. x 2 ft. x 6 ft. x 1728 cu. in. /cu. ft. = 20,736 cu. in.

Rubric: 2 possible points

1 point (content): Realize hole has no dirt in it

1 point (clarity): Explanation clearly written—this point could be awarded to a student getting an answer of 20,736 cu. in.

75. The kid was born in the Southern Hemisphere.

76. If the hour hand is pointing at 9, the minute hand should be at 12. If the minute hand is at 3, the hour hand should be a quarter of the way past 9. Assume the same relative positions of the hands.

Note: A student may say that both hands could be moved. This is a correct answer as well, as long as the hands are in the proper positions.

77. Varies

78. Varies

79. Varies

80. 15—2, 5, 8, 25, 53, 28, 82, 58, 85, 258, 285, 528, 582, 825, 852

81. Gold. The black container has 3 red marbles out of a total of 5, which is 0.6 probability for red. The gold container has 2 red marbles out of a total number of 3, which is 0.67 probability for red. Gold has a better probability of getting a red marble.

Rubric: 4 possible points

2 points (content): Computing the probability for each container

1 point (content): Knowing 0.67 > (is greater than) 0.6

1 point (clarity): Explanation clearly written

82. Varies

83. Varies

84.

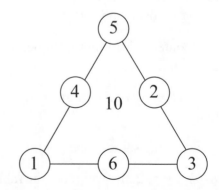

85.

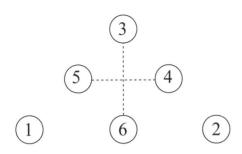

86.   5. Some student might want to count some of the partial circles and might even attempt to rationalize that they should be counted because part of the circle is hidden. The hidden partial circle idea is not supported by the picture. However, you could have an interesting discussion with the student as you ask for an explanation. That conversation could prove to be a valuable learning experience.

87.   36

88.   Varies

89.   C and D. C has no straight segments in it, as do A, B, D, and E. D has no circle, as do A, B, C, and E.

Note: If students have worked with the difference between line segments, rays, and lines, you could change the solution wording accordingly. Technically, the figures all have line segments in them, but they will often be referred to as lines because of "common" language usage.

Rubric: 2 possible points

1 point (content): Recognition of at least one of the patterns

1 point (clarity): Explanation clearly written

90.   Varies—any name that begins with E

Rubric: 2 possible points

1 point (content): Recognition of the "first letter of the name" pattern

1 point (clarity): Explanation clearly written

91.   Rearrange the 3 pens to form the sides of a new pen. See graphic below:

92.   7   .
Note: Some student might rationalize that the answer is 3 because if the 3 small squares are removed, no squares remain. The student is thinking along the line of erasing the small squares so the figure would look like the one below:

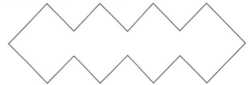

93.   30. The large square contains one 4x4 square, four 3x3 squares, nine 2x2 squares, and 16 1x1 squares, for a total of 30 squares. It is common for students to consider only the 16 small squares initially. Usually, someone will recognize the need to consider the large 4x4 square, but sometimes it takes some prompting to get them to consider the 2x2 squares. A good way to show the solution is to have a transparency of a 4x4 checkerboard and then have a 2x2 piece of colored acetate to place on the transparency and then move it around to show the nine 2x2 squares.

Rubric: 4 possible points

1 point (content): Pattern of counting four 3x3 squares

1 point (content): Pattern of counting nine 2x2 squares

1 point (content): All squares considered

1 point (clarity): Explanation clearly written

94.   5 squares (4 small ones and the one large one), 16 triangles

95.   The letters M, N, and P are moved to the new locations M, N, and P. Note that M, N, and P could be interchanged.

See graphic below:

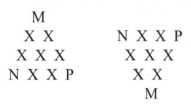

```
       M
     X X              N X X P
    X X X             X X X
   N X X P             X X
                         M
```

96.   Varies.

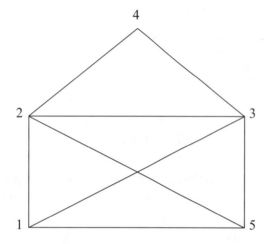

Number the vertices as shown in the picture above. One possible solution would involved starting at 1, going to 2, then 3, then 4, followed by 2, then 5, then 3, then 1, and finally 5. There are other solutions. For example, start at 5 and then go to 3 and continue by mirroring what was done in the given solution.

97.   Above the line segment. Letters composed of straight line segments go only above the line segment, and letters that have curved line segments in them go only below the line segment.

98.   5. Examples, as shown in the graphic on the next page.

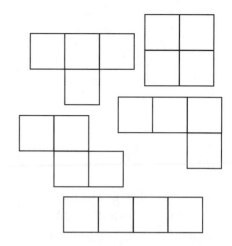

Rubric: 3 possible points

1 point (content): Correct configurations

1 point (content): All possible configurations present

1 point (clarity): Incorrect or duplicate configurations present

99.   36.

8 @ 1 by long
7 @ 2 by long
6 @ 3 by long
5 @ 4 by long
4 @ 5 by long
3 @ 6 by long
2 @ 7 by long
1 @ 8 by long

100.   Row 1: vertical symmetry

Row 2: horizontal symmetry

Row 3: both

101.   Varies. This problem has several correct answers. See below:

$$\frac{8}{4} - \frac{2}{1} = 0 \qquad\qquad \frac{2}{1} - \frac{8}{4} = 0$$

$$4 \times 2 - 8 \times 1 = 0 \qquad 8 \times 1 - 4 \times 2 = 0$$

102. Use Roman numerals and erase the shaded region. See graphic below:

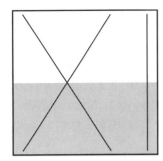

103. 5. Seven seat belts means at most, a driver + 6 kids per van. Or, one seat belt in each van is for the driver. 25/6 = 4, with a remainder of 1. That 1 kid means a fifth van is needed.

104. 26.5 square feet. Superimpose squares on the figure and count the full squares as 1 unit each. Put the triangles together to make other squares and count each of those. Finally, one triangle left is half a square. See graphic below:

This triangle is half of a square.   These two triangles together make 2.

	1	1	1			
1	1	1	1			
1	1	1	1	1	1	1
1	1	1	1	1	1	1

Each set of two triangles together makes 1.

OR

The outer region's area is 35 square feet. Find the area of the unshaded part the same way as demonstrated for finding the shaded area and subtract the unshaded parts.

Rubric: 3 possible points

1 point (content): Recognition that whole is sum of parts

1 point (content): Correct answer

1 point (clarity): Explanation clearly written

105. 1.5. A student could rationalize that something is needed so that when it is divided into thirds, the answer is a half. Money could be a useful tool to assist in solving this problem.

OR

If "it" is X, then $\frac{1}{2} = \frac{X}{3}$

Solve for X and get 1.5. Note that algebra is not necessary to solve this problem but that the basics of algebra would be used to get the solution, even if the student did not realize it.

106. Varies. A fast strategy for finding the number is always to take half of the remaining set (rounding to eliminate fractions). Suppose the chosen number is 65. Guess 50 and you will be told it is too small. You now know the mystery number is between 51 and 100 inclusive. Guess 75 and you will be told it is too large. Now you know the mystery number is between 51 and 74 inclusive. Guess 62 and you are told it is too small. You now know the mystery number is between 63 and 74 inclusive. Guess 68. Too big. Guess 65. YOU GOT IT! Using this routine, you will always get the mystery number in no more than 7 tries.

107. O. The pattern is increasing at a constant rate for each of X and O. First come one X and one O. Next come 2 Xs and 2 Os. If the pattern continues along those lines, since there are 3 Xs, the next entry should be the first of 3 Os. Either one O or 3 Os would be an acceptable response.

Rubric: 2 possible points

1 point (content): Recognition that an O comes next—note that 3 Os would be acceptable also

1 point (clarity): Explanation clearly written

108. Any animal whose name has 7 letters. The pattern is any animal with a name having 3 letters, then 4 letters, then 5 letters, then 6, etc.

Rubric: 2 possible points

1 point (content): Pattern recognition

1 point (clarity): Explanation clearly written

109.

31	17	15	1
29	19	13	3
27	21	11	5
25	23	9	7

The pattern follows vertically: columns 1 and 3 have numbers that are reduced by 2 each time; columns 2 and 4 have numbers that are increased by 2 each time.

110. 14. If the trees are on your right on the way to school, those same trees will be on your left on the way home.

Rubric: 2 possible points

1 point (content): Recognition that the same trees are being counted

1 point (clarity): Explanation clearly written

111. 3. Worst case scenario: First you pull a red sock. Next you pull a blue sock. At this point you have now pulled 2 socks and they do not match. The third sock must match either the red one or the blue one. You could pull a red sock on the first try and a red sock on the second try. If that happens, you have a matching pair, but you cannot be assured that will always happen. When pulling 3 socks, you are always guaranteed a pair.

Rubric: 2 possible points

1 point (content): Recognition that 3 socks guarantee a matching pair

1 point (clarity): Explanation clearly written

112. Any flower. The sequence is the name of any flower followed by any noun, then any flower, etc.

Rubric: 2 possible points

1 point (content): Recognition of the flower pattern

1 point (clarity): Explanation clearly written

113. Varies—any food that begins with the letter D; a 3-letter word; a 3-letter vegetable; any vegetable.

114. Any animal that does not fly OR any animal with 7 letters in its name.

Note: It is important for children to be able to adapt their thinking to follow the logic being used by another person in another situation. It is also important for them to realize that there are some problems in a mathematics class that have more than one right answer.

Rubric: 2 possible points

1 point (content): Recognition of a logical pattern used by someone else

1 point (clarity): Explanation clearly written

115. twelve plus one

116. Take out the letters "ten letters" and you are left with "an important word." This trick question can generate much discussion and stimulates divergent thinking. The objective is more than the answer.

117. T (Thirteen). Each letter is the first letter of the consecutive odd counting numbers, beginning with One (One, Three, Five, Seven, Nine, Eleven, Thirteen).

118. 9 below and 10 above. Even and odd number of letters in the spelled number name.
OR

The numbers above the segment can be determined by considering the following pattern: +1, +1, +3, +1, +1, +3, etc. where the first +1 means that 1 is added to 1 to get 2, the second number in the sequence above the segment. The second +1 means that you add 1 to the 2 to get 3, the third number in the sequence above the segment. The +3 means that you add 3 to 6 to get the next number in the sequence, 6. Then the pattern repeats so that gives the 7 and 8 above the segment. After that, the sequence would have you adding 3 to 8 to get 11 which would be the next number above the sequence. So, assuming that pattern, the 9 and 10 would be placed below the segment.

OR

The numbers below the segment have the pattern: +4, +1, +4, +1, etc. The set of numbers shown below the segment is 0, 4, 5. Add 4 to zero to get 4. Add 1 to 4 to get 5. Then repeat the pattern. Add 4 to 5 to get 9 and then add 1 to 9 to get 10. That reasoning would place the 9 and 10 below the segment.

OR

Divide the number by 5. If the remainder is 1, 2 or 3, the number goes above the segment. If the remainder is 0 or 4, the number goes below the segment.

OR

Both the 9 and the 10 should go below the segment, because the pattern is 1 down, 3 up, 2 down, 3 up, 3 down, 3 up, and so on.

Note: This is an outstanding example of how a problem can be viewed from a variety of perspectives, sometimes giving different answers and sometimes giving the same answer. This exemplifies why asking students to explain how they arrive at their conclusions can be so critical.

Rubric: 2 possible points

1 point (content): Recognize a pattern

1 point (clarity): Explanation clearly written

119. Put all the bowls inside each other and all the beans in the top bowl. There are variations of this that could be used. For example, put one bean in the smallest bowl, two in the next smallest, and 2 in the largest, still putting all the bowls inside each other. The largest bowl would hold 5 beans; two directly, none inside the next to the largest, 2 beans inside the next to the smallest bowl and 1 bean inside the smallest bowl. That means that the smallest bowl would hold an odd number of beans—1. The next smallest bowl would hold 2 directly plus the one in the smallest bowl which would be placed inside the next smallest bowl, which would mean that the total number of beans in the next smallest bowl would be odd—3. The next to the smallest bowl containing 3 beans (2 in it and 1 in the smallest bowl which is inside it) would be placed in the next to the largest bowl (which holds no beans directly in it) making the number of beans in the next to the largest bowl be odd—3.

Finally, put all 3 bowls inside the largest bowl which holds 2 beans directly and 3 more in the bowls inside it giving an odd number—5. See the Rubric on the next page.

Rubric: 2 possible points

1 point (content): Recognition of the pattern

1 point (clarity): The explanation is clearly written

120.   Varies. The concept of asking the right questions can be critical in the study of mathematics. This type of game helps children learn the skills and logic involved in questioning.

121.   t e n h o r s e s. It is spelled with 9 letters, putting one letter in each stall. This trick question has generated a lot of discussion and stimulates divergent thinking. One of the more creative answers that came from an elementary student was to arrange the 9 stalls in a circle and use the center for the 10th horse. The objective of this problem is more than the answer.

122.   3. The first number of each pair is a counting number starting with one. The second number in each pair tells the number of letters in the spelling of the counting number. For the pair (1, 3) you get that one has 3 letters, from the pair (2, 3) you get that two has 3 letters. For the pair (3, 5) you get that three has 5 letters, etc. For the pair (10, ?) you get that ten has 3 letters.

Rubric: 3 possible points

1 point (content): Pattern of counting numbers as the first member of each pair

1 point (content): Pattern of counting the number of letters in the number word

1 point (clarity): Explanation clearly written

123.   3. The digits are the ones found with those letters on the telephone key pad.

124.   Each word in the sentence has one letter more than the last word.

Rubric: 3 possible points

1 point (content): Pattern of increasing number of letters in words

1 point (content): Correct counting of number of letters in words

1 point (clarity): Explanation clearly written

125.   One thousand.

Note: Some students say 101 as "One hundred and one" and they might want to use that as the answer. However, "One hundred and one" is an improper expression and must be discounted.

126.   14. Count the letters in the number word of each of the given numbers. The number of letters increases by one as you go from left to right. That is, ten is spelled with 3 letters, four is spelled with 4 letters, three has 5 letters, etc.